Zeke Goes to Space School

Zeke　Blip　Mr Moon

Written by Jill McDougall
Illustrated by Tom Bonson

This is Zeke.

He lives on a planet far away.

It is his first day at Space School.

"Do I *have* to go?" asked Zeke.

"I will not have any friends at Space School."

"It will be fine," said Mum.

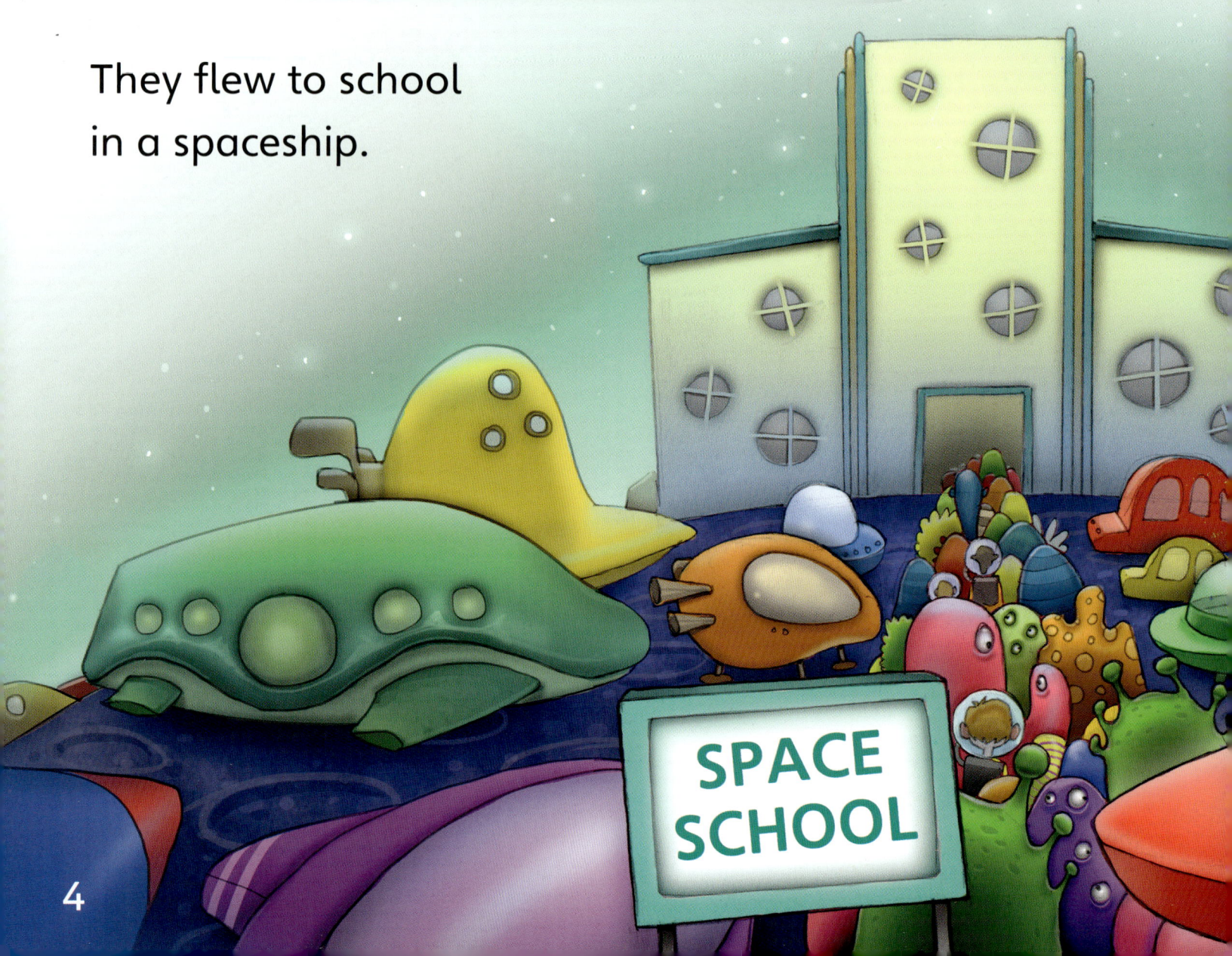

They flew to school in a spaceship.

"Come in, Zeke," said Mr Moon.

"There are lots of things to do."

Some aliens were playing with slime.

"Can I play?" asked Zeke.

"Yes," they said.

The slime was sticky.
"Yuck!" said Zeke.

Some aliens were playing with funny hats, but there were no hats for Zeke.

Zeke was sad.

He sat down on a rug.

"Hello!" said the rug.

The rug was an alien!

"My name is Blip," said the alien.
"I will play with you."

Zeke and Blip made a rocket.

"Can we play?" asked some aliens.

"Yes," said Blip. "Come in!"

Mum came to pick up Zeke from school.

"Did you make some friends today?" she asked.

"I made *lots* of friends," said Zeke.